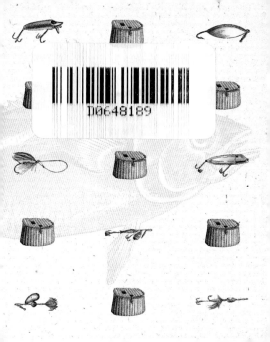

I0648189

FISHING
An Angler's Miscellany

Edited by Mark Hoff

Ariel Books

Andrews and McMeel
Kansas City

Frontispiece: A. Rowland Knight, active 1893-1926

ISBN: 0-8362-3117-1

Library of Congress Catalog Card Number: 94-74180

CONTENTS

INTRODUCTION

Fishing has always been more than simply a sport. It originated together with hunting as a means for humans to get food for survival. And because fishing, like hunting, is an activity that measures success in terms of one's ability to capture a wild animal, fishing is full of hazards. For commercial fishermen who make their living from the sea, fishing is a sometimes dangerous and difficult way of life that offers unstable financial returns. For sport fishermen who fish for enjoyment, angling is a hobby that tempers every reward with large doses of frustration, disappointment, and general hard knocks.

Why, then, do people fish? Why is it that throughout the world anglers can be seen waiting expectantly at water's edge as hook and line disappear into the dark depths below? The question has no single answer—or none that all anglers would accept. People fish for food, for relaxation, or for the simple challenge of catching "the big one." Yet fishing's most universal appeal is perhaps its inescapable mystery. Like few other sports, fishing puts a person into direct contact with nature. Humans can never be at home in the water, but they can experience another world of sorts and seek answers to ineffable questions there. Thus, every fishing trip is a kind of voyage of discovery into that mysterious "other" world, and every catch is a kind of message from the deep.

THE HISTORY
OF FISHING

Fishing is one of the most ancient of all
human activities. It is most simply defined
as the sport of catching fish by means
of a hook. Angling, a traditional

and more poetic term, gets its name from the hook, or "angle," employed in the activity.

Fishing probably dates from the Stone Age. While the first fisherman was probably a hunter in search of an easier way of capturing his elusive underwater prey than spearing it, no one knows exactly when the world's first fisherman baited a primitive hook and threw a line into the water. However, all anglers can agree that the magic moment when fishing was brought into the world was a happy one indeed for the human race.

Hooks

In its beginning, fishing was simply a means of snaring fish with a hook and line. The simple hook is thus the crux of the matter—it certainly is for the fish! The first hook was not really a hook but a gorge, a curved object made of a piece of bone or stone that a fish could swallow together with the bait and line. The gorge would stick in the fish's throat or stomach when the fisher pulled on the line.

Fishhooks evolved gradually to take on the distinctive curved shape we know today. The discovery and use of metal made fashioning a hook easier than carving one from bone or wood. Copper was used for hooks as early as 5000 B.C. When Bronze Age metal-smiths learned to mix tin with copper about 4000 B.C., they applied their knowledge to making fishhooks. It was about this time that hooks were barbed and enhanced with an eye for tying the line. Iron was probably used for fishhooks by about 2000 B.C., and well before the time of Christ steel hooks were used around the Mediterranean.

Steel hooks evolved slowly, and the fore-runners of the modern fishhook industry began in London during the 1600s. By about 1650 Charles Kirby produced a hook pattern with what became known as the "Kirby bend." It has been commonly used ever since. The center of the hook industry then moved from England to Norway, where by

1832 the famous hook manufacturing company Mustad and Sons was established.

Lines

The first fishing line was probably made from the vine of a plant. Later lines were constructed by braiding horsehair or even human hair. Hair lines proved to be quite strong and were used up through the mid-1800s. By the late 1800s, horsehair lines were replaced by those made of silk covered with several coats of linseed oil. These new lines could be cast roughly three times farther than the old ones. Silk lines also made it possible for anglers to perfect fly-fishing methods. In the twentieth century, the invention of plastic-coated fly lines and nylon monofilament lines for spin fishing revolutionized fishing tackle. The new equipment began to be mass produced after World War II and made quality fishing tackle inexpensive.

Rods and Reels

The first fishing was done with merely a line and hook thrown by hand, but this limited anglers to fishing from a boat or an unobstructed bank. The first rod was probably a tree branch or stick used by an angler to hold his line over bushes or other obstacles on shore. For thousands of years the fishing rod remained short by modern standards, only about a yard long. This kind of rod is pictured in ancient Egyptian and Chinese drawings of fishermen. References in Roman writings show that a longer, jointed rod was in use by the fourth century A.D. in the Roman Empire.

So far as we can tell, the rod did not evolve much until the beginning of the modern era. In the seventeenth century the British began to experiment with rod technology. Wire rings were attached to the end of rods, which increased the angler's control over the line. Lines were still relatively short, however—about twenty-five yards at most. The invention of the looped rod tip created another problem—namely, how to prevent the new, longer lines from tangling. The answer, which was developed over centuries, was the reel.

The first reel, probably invented by the ancient Chinese, was a kind of wooden spool patterned after a bobbin. British reels in the 1600s were equipped with a metal ring the angler placed around his thumb to control the line. Later reels were equipped with handles that moved the spool to take in or let out line. In the United States, reel technology was led by two Kentucky watchmakers who decided to produce and market reels for bait casting. In 1810 George Snyder made the first multiplying reel, an entirely handcrafted machine. Jonathan Meek then went into the reel-making business, improving on Snyder's designs and creating a new craze for bait casting.

As reel manufacturing slowly improved, so did rod technology. Rod makers experimented with exotic woods, which were lighter and more elastic than the woods then in use. First, such woods as lancewood and greenheart were imported from South America, but then bamboo from Asia was found to be the most promising material, for it was light, strong, and flexible. By 1800 rod makers had discovered how to cut bamboo into thin strips and glue them together, thus creating a thinner and lighter rod that was still strong and flexible. Rod makers continued to experiment with bamboo, especially in the United States and Great Britain. By about 1870 hexagonal bamboo rods were made by laminating six pieces of finely cut triangular pieces of bamboo.

The development of such materials as fiberglass, aluminum, and graphite in the twentieth century changed fishing rods in ways that would have astounded anglers from previous centuries. The new synthetic materials allowed rods to become shorter, lighter, and stronger than earlier wooden rods. Split bamboo was replaced in all but a few rods first by fiberglass and then by synthetic materials like graphite and boron. The up-to-date angler uses fishing tackle made from some of the same space-age materials that go into space stations.

However, the sport remains the same in its essentials as it did in the beginning: the angler still has to hook the elusive fish and land it in his net.

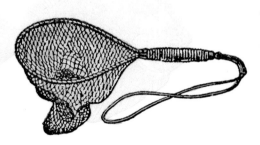

FISHY QUOTES

Something within fishermen tries to make fishing into a world perfect and apart.

—*Norman Maclean*

Fishing is a delusion entirely surrounded by liars in old clothes.

—*Don Marquis*

A hook's well lost to catch a salmon.

—*Anonymous*

The charm of fishing is that it is the pursuit of what is elusive but obtainable, a perpetual series of occasions for hope.

—*John Buchan*

I really fished mainly because I wanted to be alone on the middle of the lake. . . . Sometimes a fish jumped nearby, as though it knew it was safe.

—*Susan Allen Toth*

It always was the biggest fish I caught that got away.

—*Eugene Field*

Of all the world's enjoyments
    That ever valued were,
There's none of our employments
    With fishing can compare.

—*Thomas D'Urfey*

The curious thing about fishing is you never want to go home. If you catch something, you can't stop. If you don't catch anything, you hate to leave in case something might bite.

—*Gladys Taber*

The sea has never been friendly to man. At most it has been the accomplice of human restlessness.

—*Joseph Conrad*

My brother and I would have preferred to start learning how to fish by going out and catching a few. . . . But it wasn't by way of fun that we were introduced to our father's art. If our father had had his say, nobody who did not know how to fish would be allowed to disgrace a fish by catching him.

—*Norman Maclean*

You must lose a fly to catch a trout.

—*George Herbert*

Fish must swim thrice—once in the water,
a second time in the sauce, and a third time
in wine in the stomach.

—*John Ray*

Whenever I find myself growing grim about
the mouth; whenever it is a damp, drizzly
November in my soul—then I account it
high time to get to sea as soon as I can.

—*Herman Melville*

All that are lovers of virtue, and dare trust
in his Providence, and be quiet and
go a-angling.

—Izaak Walton

The man who goes fishing gets something
more than the fish he catches.

—Mary Astor

The brain gives up a lot less easily than the body, so fly-fishermen have developed what they call the "curiosity theory," which is about what it says it is. It is the theory that fish, like men, will sometimes strike at things just to find out what they are and not because they look good to eat. With most fly-fishermen it is the "last resort theory," but it sometimes almost works.

—*Norman Maclean*

Give me mine angle, we'll to the river;
    there,
My music playing far off, I will betray
Tawny-finn'd fishes; my bended hook shall
    pierce
Their slimy jaws.

    —*William Shakespeare*

Fly-fishing may be a very pleasant
amusement; but angling or float fishing
I can only compare to a stick and a
string, with a worm at one end and a fool
at the other.

    —*Dr. Samuel Johnson*

An employment for my idle time, which is
then not idly spent.

—*Sir Henry Wotton*

The gods do not deduct from man's allotted
span the hours spent in fishing.

—*Babylonian proverb*

As no man is born an artist, so no man is born an angler.

—*Izaak Walton*

A stream is music and motion: smooth glides, fast, turbulent riffles and deep pools, each posing a special challenge.

—*Nelson Bryant*

It is impossible to avoid the conclusion that the fishing habit, by promoting close association with nature, by teaching patience, and by generating or stimulating useful contemplation, tends directly to the increase of the intellectual power of its votaries and through them to the improvement of our national character.

—*Grover Cleveland*

Something odd, detached, and even slightly humorous happens to a big-fish fisherman a moment after a big fish strikes. In the arm, shoulder, or brain of a big-fish fisherman is a scale, and the moment the big fish goes in the air the big-fish fisherman, no matter what his blood pressure is, places the scale under the fish and coolly weighs him.

—*Norman Maclean*

Oh, give me grace to catch a fish
So big that even I
When talking of it afterwards
May have no need to lie.

—*Anonymous*

All men are equal before fish.

—*Herbert Hoover*

Poets talk about "spots of time," but it is really fishermen who experience eternity compressed into a moment. No one can tell what a spot of time is until suddenly the whole world is a fish and the fish is gone.

—Norman Maclean

To capture the fish is not all of the fishing.

—Zane Grey

You will find angling to be like the virtue of humility, which has a calmness of spirit and a world of other blessings attending upon it.

—*Izaak Walton*

All you need to be a fisherman is patience and a worm.

—*Herb Shriner*

A rest to my mind, a cheerer of my spirits, a diverter of sadness, a calmer of unquiet thoughts, a moderator of passions, a procurer of contentedness.

—*Sir Henry Wotton*

Fishing is much more than fish. . . . It is the great occasion when we may return to the fine simplicity of our forefathers.

—*Herbert Hoover*

One great thing about fly-fishing is that after a while nothing exists of the world but thoughts about fly-fishing.

—*Norman Maclean*

FISHING: An Angler's Miscellany

When the wind is in the East,
Then the fishes bite the least;
When the wind is in the West,
Then the fishes bite the best;
When the wind is in the North,
Then the fishes do come forth;
When the wind is in the South,
It blows the bait in the fish's mouth.

—*Old English rhyme*

THREE WAYS
TO CATCH A FISH

As every class-conscious socialite knows, society has been traditionally divided into three levels: upper, middle, and lower. The educated angler knows that the fishing world is similarly ordered according to three distinct types: fly-fishermen, spin fishermen, and bait fishermen.

While representatives of each angler class often claim not to have any interest in the activities of the other two, most fishermen have tried their hands at various types of fishing. Even the raretied fly-fisherman, presumed aristocrat though he may be, probably had his first fishing experience with bait fishing. This is especially true in the United States, where fly-fishermen tend to work their way "up" to their sport via the so-called "lower" forms of fishing. In Great Britain, fly-fishermen traditionally belong to the upper classes or have the means to afford the considerable expenses involved in buying equipment and fishing time on privately owned trout and salmon rivers.

Fly-Fishing

Fly-fishermen are the aristocrats of the sport; theirs is the most sophisticated, difficult, and, generally, expensive form of fishing. The fly-fisherman fishes with flies made to resemble insects or baitfish, tied with thread, animal hair, and other strange products. He waves his rod through the air, creating vast loops of line, and attempts to place his fly over the nose of a feeding fish. As might be expected, the prey of choice for most fly-fishermen are the aristocrats of the aquatic world: the high-strung trout or noble salmon. Between them and all other practitioners of the sport, so fly-fishermen insist, is a world of difference.

Spin Fishing

Spin fishermen are the steady middle-class representatives of the sport. Spin fishing is a method of casting a lure with a relatively short, flexible rod and a fixed-spool reel. Virtually all fish may be pursued by the spin fisherman—from trout to bonefish. Spin fishing is versatile, no-nonsense, and highly democratic, for it is relatively easy to learn and inexpensive to pursue.

Bait Fishing

Finally, bait fishermen make up the proletarian base of fishing society. Bait fishing is the archetypal standard of fishing everywhere, a throwback to the dawn of the sport when Stone Age men tossed meat on a wooden gorge into the water. As with spin fishing, virtually all fish may be pursued by the bait fisherman. It is bait fishing that most nonfishermen call to mind when the subject of fishing comes up.

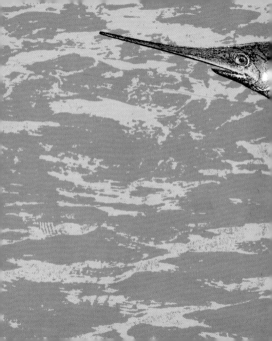

BIG-GAME FISHING

If fly-fishing is the most aristocratic form of angling, then big-game fishing is the most macho form. It refers to the pursuit of large marine game fish—such as marlin, swordfish, tuna, and tarpon—and bears as much resemblance to the delicacies of presenting feather-light flies to finicky trout as fencing does to heavyweight boxing.

The International Game Fish Association, established in 1939, promotes big-game fishing and supervises fishing competitions, creating weight categories for lines and keeping championship records. It also promotes the study of game fish through the tagging and releasing of select fish and encourages the conservation of endangered species.

The Tuna That Started It All

Big-game fishing got its start as a recognized U.S. sport when Charles Holder shocked the fishing world by catching a 183-pound bluefin tuna off California's Catalina Island on June 1, 1898. Prior to this, it had been thought that such deep-water fish as tuna, which can swim extremely fast and dive deep, could never be caught with a rod and reel. Holder's boat capsized once during the 3 3/4-hour fight, but he held on and managed to get back on the boat to continue the battle.

Holder formed the Catalina Tuna Club that same month, and big-game fishing took off. The club's rules stipulated that tuna must be caught with a rod and reel on line no stronger than seventy-two–pound test. Such tackle restrictions would become a sporting tradition.

Club membership grew quickly. By the end of the month following its founding, the club boasted twenty-four members who had caught tuna weighing more than 100 pounds. Since these catches were well-publicized, wealthy sportsmen everywhere began taking up the new sport. Club members wore special buttons indicating their catches, and soon such marks of fishing prowess only added to the competitive spirit. One British angler/writer complained after visiting the club that the desire to acquire the buttons spoiled the

FISHING: An Angler's Miscellany

true fishing spirit, but big-game catches continued to be measured and weighed and fishermen continued to vie for the largest prizes.

The early days of big-game fishing were the domain of wealthy anglers. Deep-sea fishing boats were not readily available for hire in those days, so the pioneers of the sport were those who could buy, outfit, and maintain their own. The first big-game fishermen were often colorful tycoons or wealthy self-made men, most of whom were early members of the Catalina Tuna Club. The most famous of them, and one of the century's most avid anglers, was the Western writer Zane Grey.

Zane Grey

Although Zane Grey endured years as the proverbial struggling writer, after 1912, when he published *Riders of the Purple Sage*, his fortune was made. With his new wealth and freedom, Grey decided to go fishing. In fact, he did it for the rest of his life—and he didn't quit until a series of heart attacks (one of which he suffered while fishing) laid him low.

Grey went in search of big-game fish throughout the world. When in 1924 he caught the first "giant" big-game fish—a 758-pound bluefin tuna off Yarmouth, Nova Scotia—interest in big-game fishing exploded. Grey became vice president of the

Catalina Tuna Club. He outfitted a 190-foot boat and took it to the Galápagos, New Zealand, and Tahiti. Grey became the first man to catch a 1,000-pound-plus fish on a rod and reel (a 1,040-pound Pacific blue marlin). At one time he held over a dozen saltwater world records. These included a 758-pound bluefin tuna, a 111-pound yellowtail, a 450-pound striped marlin, a 1,036-pound tiger shark, and a 482-pound swordfish. And, of course, he wrote about his exploits in fishing and sporting magazines.

Grey also revolutionized big-game fishing in other ways. He pioneered the use of light tackle, in the interest of making such fishing more sporting. He went in search of fish other anglers had not thought to pursue, such as the permit and bonefish. And he advocated conservation, warning against commercial overfishing and advocating the release of healthy game fish. But Grey ran afoul of the rules and regulations of big-game fishing. Once when he was battling a swordfish he suggested that his reel, which had frozen up, be cut off and his line tied to a new reel. The boat captain said that such a switch would violate the rules and thus disqualify the fish for the Tuna Club's records. Grey wrote later: "I do not fish for clubs or records. I fish for the fun, the excitement, the thrill of the game, and I would rather let my fish go than not."

STRANGE BUT TRUE
FISHING TALES

Presidential Mishaps

During an August 1989 fishing vacation in Maine, avid fisherman George Bush went catchless for seventeen straight days—and it all happened in the public eye. Reporters and photographers followed the president wherever he went in his twenty-eight-foot cigarette boat, *Fidelity*. A "fish watch" was created by the *Portland Press Herald*, which used a bluefish with a red line through it to indicate each zero-fish day. Reporters were seen wearing improvised press credentials with a "no fish" logo, and when they caught bluefish in their own boats, they held them up for the envious president to see. Finally, on the eighteenth, and last, day of his vacation, Bush appealed for divine help by praying at St. Ann's Episcopal Church. That day Bush caught a 10-pound bluefish on a jawbuster lure. Reporters and Secret Service agents in nearby boats cheered, and back at the dock the president was greeted by a celebration more befitting an election-night victory than a triumph over a lone bluefish.

Richard Nixon was without doubt one of the worst fishermen ever to inhabit the White House. In 1952, when future president Dwight Eisenhower invited his running mate to go fly-fishing, Nixon proved to be all thumbs when it came to mastering the intricacies of casting a fly. On Nixon's first cast he hooked a tree limb. As Ike patiently explained the motions of fly casting, Nixon gritted his teeth and cast again—only to hook the same branch. Nixon cast a third time and hooked Eisenhower on the shirt. The great general, who had led the Allies to victory in World War II, was forced to admit defeat before Nixon's clumsiness. Nixon later noted that Ike was clearly disappointed and never asked him to go fishing again.

President Calvin Coolidge didn't allow his lack of angling ability to ruin his enjoyment of the sport. After returning from a fishing trip he was asked whether he had any success. Silent Cal replied, "I estimate that there are forty-five thousand fish in the river, and although I've caught hardly any of them, I've intimidated them."

Moneyed Fish That Got Away

A. Ray Cockrell is probably the only fisherman who not only ate his world-record catch but also gave away two other record-size fish and threw back three potential record holders. Cockrell was surf fishing in Destin, Florida, on

June 3, 1988, when one gigantic bluefish after another struck his bait. Cockrell laid the huge blues on the beach, where they soon attracted a crowd. Cockrell threw three fish back, gave two others away, and kept the largest. It weighed in at a whopping 42 pounds—more than 10 pounds over the world record. Unfortunately, no one told him it was a record-class fish. So Cockrell took his fish home and ate it. A representative of the International Game Fish Association visited Cockrell later to tell him what the world record was. Cockrell would have made the record books in two categories for his fish, and he had ignored a grand total of six potential world-record fish.

In 1986 Fred Holland was one of 6,212 contestants in the largest and richest fishing contest in the world: the Arthur Smith King Mackerel Tournament in South Carolina. Holland pulled in a monster king of about 50 pounds—an almost certain winner for the $60,000 prize for the biggest kingfish.

When Holland pulled up at the dock to weigh his fish, enthusiastic spectators called out for him to display his sure winner. Holland obliged, lifting the fish over his head to show off for the cameras. As he did so, the huge king slipped out of his hands, fell to the dock, and bounced into the water. Everyone looked down into the water for a sign of the fish, sure it would reappear. Arthur Smith encouraged Holland, saying, "Don't give up hope—dead fish usually float, don't they?" But Holland's did not. He raced up and down the dock in desperation, searching for some sign of his $60,000 fish. He even hired scuba divers to search for the king. It was never found.

Bad Karma

Paul Clause was fishing for blue marlin off Hawaii with Capt. Glenn Van Valin in his boat *Karma* when he hooked a large marlin that gave him the ride of his life. Clause fought the marlin for two hours and was able to bring the fish close enough to the boat to gaff it. He remained seated in the fighting chair as Van Valin reached down to gaff the magnificent fish. Clause remembers seeing an explosion of fish and water and feeling a powerful jerk. The next thing he knew he was flying through the air, grabbing anything in sight in an attempt to save his life. Seconds later he was being pulled deep underwater, still strapped to the chair. In its powerful burst to get away, the marlin had ripped the fighting chair, together with the four-by-six-foot engine cover, from its moorings on the boat—and Clause was being pulled down to an almost certain death. Fortunately, he had not secured his safety belt and had loosened the harness straps. He was able to free himself at a depth of about eighty feet and swam back to the boat. Clause was underwater more than a minute and a half, and his inner ears were filled with water, but he was lucky to be alive. After he had revived, Clause reportedly told Van Valin, "Now I know how a fish feels when it's hooked."

The Perils of "Noodling"

Master noodler John Pidcock noodled his largest catfish in July 1993 from an abandoned beaver hole in the Deep Fork River, Oklahoma. Pidcock found a dark tunnel in the beaver hole and crawled into it head-first. Two of his friends stood behind him, holding onto his feet. Pidcock found a huge catfish at the end of the tunnel. When the cornered fish bit him on the hand, Pidcock reached into its mouth, grabbed the fish by its thick lower lip, held on as tight as he could, and signaled his friends to pull him out. The catfish weighed 48 pounds. Pidcock, who had his finger broken from that bite, nonetheless enjoys his sport: "There's nothing more gratifying than getting bit by a big catfish. The adrenaline rush is unbelievable."

Braggers Beware

Mark Twain, an avid hunter and fisherman, enjoyed telling of his exploits. Once, returning by train from a three-week fishing trip in Maine, he picked the wrong target for his boasting. The fish iced and stowed in the baggage car, Twain related the tale of his very successful off-season catch to a fellow passenger. Pausing in his monologue, he asked the stranger who he was. The man said, "I'm the state game warden. And who are you?" Twain recovered enough to say with conviction, "I'm the biggest liar in the whole United States!"

GLOSSARY OF
FISHING TERMS

Chuck and Chance It: This term refers to careless or sloppy fishing, when an angler simply fishes the water with an inappropriate fly, relying on blind luck more than anything else.

Dapping: This is the delicate art of fishing for trout by dangling on the water's surface a fly attached to a clear monofilament line. The practice dates back at least to about 1300, when the word *dab* was first used in England to describe this kind of fishing.

Duffer's Fortnight: In Great Britain this is the two-week period in late May and/or early June when brown trout come up in droves to feed on the mayflies that cover the water's surface. Tradition holds that during this period the trout are particularly easy to catch.

Foul Hooking: This term refers to catching a fish that is hooked anywhere but in the mouth. Sometimes the hook falls out of the fish's mouth and catches on a fin or elsewhere in the body. Landing a foul-hooked fish is considered bad form (some anglers think it brings bad luck), and regulations in some areas require the release of foul-hooked fish.

Garden Fly: This euphemistic term is used to refer to the worm unscrupulous fishermen use to take salmon illegally from fly-only waters. Use of the garden fly is shunned by law-abiding fly-fishermen.

Gillie: This is an assistant or guide to a fisherman. The gillie is often a skilled fisherman himself but generally remains in the background to offer advice and assistance (similar to a caddie in golf).

Gut-Shy: A fish that is wary of a fly-fisherman's leader is gut-shy. The term dates from the time before the invention of nylon monofilament line when leaders were made of fine gut, and fish that refused to take flies because they could see the gut leader on the water were termed gut-shy.

Hands: A fisherman who is particularly skillful in casting and playing fish is said to have good hands or, simply, hands.

Lunker: A lunker is an extraordinarily large fish—a whopper. The term is often used to refer to huge brown trout that lurk in the deepest pools of a river. It derives from an old American term meaning "stupid" or "thick-headed," although lunker brown trout are anything but stupid—dumb fish as a rule don't live long enough to attain large size.

Matching the Hatch: When a trout fisherman copies the natural flies that are hatching in the water, he is said to be matching the hatch. It can be difficult and frustrating when the fisherman doesn't have flies of the correct pattern, size, and color.

Noodling: This is the practice of diving or wading into water and wrestling large catfish out. Noodlers usually go after large catfish during spawning season, when the usually placid fish can be provoked into attacking. Once a noodler gets the fish to bite, he puts his hands into the fish's mouth and yanks it out of its hole. Often assistants with rope are needed to help pull the noodler and attached catfish out of the water. Noodling is illegal in some places, so "noodlers" tend to be surreptitious. However, in many southern states, noodling is legal and popular.

Play: This term refers to manipulating a fish after it is hooked and while it fights to free itself. Playing a fish is an art in itself and varies according to the type of fish. Playing small trout or panfish is a delicate task of seconds or minutes, while playing large game fish such as salmon or marlin can require hours of exhausting work.

Priest: This is a euphemistic term for a weighted wood or metal club used to kill a landed fish. It is said to derive from the fact that the club "administers the last rites" to the fish. In Ireland, the club is called a priest because it's the last thing the fish sees before it dies.

Rise: Rise is the movement of a fish, especially a trout, as it feeds on the surface. Every fisherman gets excited by the sight of rising fish—proof that fish are present and feeding.

Strike: This term refers to the action of raising or jerking a fishing rod upward to set the hook in the mouth of a fish that has taken a fly, lure, or bait. Striking a fish correctly is a difficult art, for an incorrect strike will pull the hook out of a fish's mouth. A strike also refers to the moment when a fish first hits the fly, lure, or bait.

Stripping: Stripping involves retrieving a lure or fly after it has been cast by pulling in line with short, rapid jerks. Stripping is usually intended to imitate the movement of a panicked baitfish, and it often excites game fish to take a fly or lure.

Window: This is the circular area through which a fish looks up at the world from under the surface of the water. Outside of this "window" the fish sees a "mirror" in which the water surface reflects everything below it.